Original title:
Aurora of Us

Copyright © 2024 Swan Charm
All rights reserved.

Author: Olivia Orav
ISBN HARDBACK: 978-9908-1-2683-8
ISBN PAPERBACK: 978-9908-1-2684-5
ISBN EBOOK: 978-9908-1-2685-2

Where Day Meets Night

The sun dips low, a golden hue,
Whispers fade as shadows grow.
Stars awake in twilight's sigh,
Where day meets night, dreams fly.

Awakening Whispers of Togetherness

Gentle breezes brush our skin,
In silence, new stories begin.
Fingers entwined, soft hearts beat,
Awakening whispers make us complete.

Brilliance in Our Shadows

In shadows cast, a light does gleam,
Reflecting hopes, a shared dream.
Through darkest nights, we find the way,
Brilliance in our shadows will stay.

A Journey Through Radiance

With every step, we chase the light,
In vibrant colors, hearts take flight.
Together we wander, hand in hand,
A journey through radiance, so grand.

Palette of Our Dreams

Colors blend in twilight's sigh,
Brush of hope upon the sky.
Waves of whispers dance in air,
Painting dreams beyond compare.

Stars awaken, softly gleam,
Shadows weave in fantasy's seam.
A palette bright, with hues so bold,
Stories of the heart unfold.

In every shade, a tale untold,
Journeying through the brave and old.
Crafting visions, vivid, clear,
A masterpiece that draws us near.

Voices echo in a gentle tune,
Underneath the silver moon.
Each stroke sings of what can be,
In our hearts, the colors free.

Ascendancy of the Light

Hear the dawn, a soft embrace,
Sunrise spills on every face.
Hope ascends with every ray,
Guiding us along our way.

Shadows fade, the dark retreats,
Brightening all the world it meets.
In the glow, we find our chance,
Life anew in radiant dance.

Hearts ignited, spirits soar,
In the light, we seek for more.
Hands united, courage grows,
In the brilliance, love bestows.

Moments shine, forever bright,
In the magic of the light.
Together we will rise again,
In the warmth, where love has been.

The Radiance Within

Deep inside, a flicker glows,
Quiet strength that gently shows.
In the silence, truth reveals,
The light of hope, our hearts it heals.

Like a candle in the night,
Guiding paths with softest light.
Within the soul, a fire burns,
For every heart, the light returns.

In twilight's calm, we find our way,
Each step forward, come what may.
Embracing shadows, still we shine,
The radiance that is divine.

Look within, and you will see,
The glow of what you're meant to be.
In unity, we let it flow,
Transforming lives with each bright glow.

Unity in the Awakening

Together we rise, hand in hand,
Awakening dreams across the land.
Voices blend in harmony,
Creating waves of unity.

In every heart, a spark ignites,
Gentle whispers of new heights.
Courage blooms as one we stand,
Building bridges, heart to hand.

As dawn breaks on our shared fate,
Endless love, we celebrate.
In the warmth of shared embrace,
We find strength in every space.

Awakening to what is true,
Beneath the sky, a vibrant hue.
In union's glow, we will ascend,
Together always, in the end.

Colors of Connection

In hues of red, we find our fire,
A bond that grows, a shared desire.
Through shades of blue, our stories flow,
In purple dreams, our spirits glow.

Green fields embrace our laughter's sound,
While golden moments, together found.
With every color, hearts align,
In vibrant strokes, our souls entwine.

Awakening Hearts

Morning breaks, the world alive,
With whispered hopes, our dreams revive.
In gentle breaths, we find our way,
To cherish love with each new day.

The warmth of sun on tender skin,
A dance that beckons us within.
As shadows fade, our spirits rise,
In harmony beneath clear skies.

Light in Our Shadows

Even in darkness, hope prevails,
A flicker bright when courage fails.
With every step, through trials we roam,
In uncertain paths, we find our home.

Illuminated by hearts so kind,
Resilience blooms, no longer blind.
Together we rise, our spirits soar,
Finding strength in love, forevermore.

Symphony of First Light

Dawn's embrace, a sweet refrain,
Soft melodies in morning's gain.
The rustling leaves join in the song,
As nature hums, we all belong.

A chorus rich of life and love,
In swirling clouds that drift above.
Each note a whisper, pure and bright,
Together we dance in first light.

When Shadows Meet Sunrise

In the hush of dawn's embrace,
Shadows twirl in soft ballet,
Whispers of the night retreat,
Bathed in the light of day.

Colors bloom in gentle grace,
Casting dreams on waking clay,
A tapestry of warmth and hope,
Where night and morn hold sway.

Silhouettes dissolve to gold,
As sunbeams chase the dark away,
Moments fleeting, beauty bold,
In the dawn's warm display.

Nature's breath begins to rise,
Birds awaken, songs convey,
Life emerges from the cold,
In harmony's bright array.

As the shadows fade and flee,
New beginnings start to play,
With each dawn a chance to see,
The magic in each day.

Threads of Daybreak

Golden threads spin through the sky,
Weaving light in colors bright,
Morning dances, soft and shy,
Chasing dreams into the light.

Mountains whisper to the streams,
As the world begins to wake,
Nature hums in gentle themes,
A fresh canvas to remake.

Clouds float by with ease and grace,
Painting hues of pink and blue,
Every heartbeat finds its place,
In the morn's refreshing view.

Time slips gently like a sigh,
Moments drift without a break,
In this quiet, dreams fly high,
Awakening with each mistake.

Threads of day in bright array,
Knit together peace and joy,
With the dawn, we find our way,
All our hopes we will employ.

Echoes in the Twilight

Twilight whispers soft and low,
As the sun bows to the night,
Stars emerge, a subtle glow,
Painting shadows with delight.

Dreamers stroll on paths of dusk,
Lost in thoughts that gently sway,
In the silence, hearts discuss,
What the fading light must say.

Crickets sing their evening song,
While the wind begins to play,
Nature's rhythm, a sweet throng,
In the twilight's soft ballet.

Colors blur then fade away,
As the night claims its own fate,
In the stillness, we shall stay,
Held in twilight's tender state.

Echoes linger, soft and sweet,
Reminders of the day's embrace,
In the hush, our lives repeat,
Finding solace in this space.

Dancing with the New Horizon

Footprints trace the edge of light,
Where the sky meets land anew,
Every step ignites the night,
Guiding dreams that will come true.

Horizons stretch with promise clear,
Whispers of the distance call,
As the dawn begins to steer,
Each heartbeat echoes through it all.

With the sun, we rise and spin,
Embrace the warmth, let shadows fade,
Life anew begins to win,
In the colors softly laid.

Dancing to the morning tune,
Hearts entwined in vibrant glow,
As the stars retreat too soon,
In the light, we find our flow.

Each horizon beckons bright,
A canvas waiting to ignite,
In the dance of day and night,
We embrace the new daylight.

Light in Our Hearts

In the dawn's gentle embrace,
A spark ignites within our souls,
Guiding us through life's vast space,
With warmth that endlessly consoles.

Flickering flames of love arise,
In shadows, they will brightly dance,
Illuminating our dark skies,
In every whispered, fleeting chance.

Together we chase distant dreams,
With hearts ablaze, we take our flight,
Through rivers deep and silver streams,
Shining like stars in the night.

The glow of hope, a steadfast guide,
In moments bright, in trials stark,
We carry light, our hearts abide,
A beacon's flame, a guiding spark.

So let us weave our tales tonight,
In unity, we stand apart,
For every journey, wrong or right,
Begins with light within our hearts.

Serendipity of Sunshine

A golden ray breaks through the grey,
It dances on the morning dew,
Whispers of joy on a sunny day,
Brightening skies with a vibrant hue.

Paths untrodden, we shall find,
In fleeting moments, chance does play,
The warmth of laughter intertwined,
As serendipity finds its way.

Fields of daisies stretch ahead,
Waving softly in the breeze,
New memories waiting to be fed,
Underneath the whimsical trees.

Every encounter, a gift bestowed,
In simple joys, we come alive,
Life's sweetest songs, the heart's abode,
In sunny moments, we will thrive.

So let us bask in this embrace,
With open hearts and arms so wide,
For every pattern, every trace,
Is painted by the sun's sweet guide.

Blooming Nocturne

In shadows deep, the night unfolds,
Whispers of dreams begin to brew,
Underneath the moon's soft hold,
The world awakes, a vibrant view.

Stars bloom bright in velvet skies,
A nocturne sung by hearts that soar,
With every twang of lullabies,
We find the peace we longed for more.

Petals dance in the evening air,
Filling our senses, pure delight,
The fragrance of hope everywhere,
In this blooming serenade of night.

A symphony of silence plays,
Embracing all who seek to dream,
In this canvas of soft grays,
Life's colors shine, a gentle gleam.

Let us wander through this space,
With eyes upturned to skies above,
For in the night, we find our place,
In blooming nocturnes, we find love.

Radiant Journeys

With every step we take anew,
The path reveals what lies ahead,
Through trials faced with hearts most true,
A tapestry of dreams is spread.

The sun arises at dawn's first light,
In every shadow, hope will rise,
Together onward, hearts ignite,
To chase the horizons of our skies.

Mountains high and valleys deep,
We journey forth, hand in hand,
Through whispers of the paths we keep,
In radiant stories, we take a stand.

The echoes of laughter fill the air,
Each moment cherished, never missed,
For as we venture, love we share,
Creating memories, too sweet to resist.

So let us roam beneath the stars,
With open hearts and eager minds,
For every journey, near or far,
Is painted bright as love unwinds.

Threads of Illumination

In the quiet we listen,
Soft whispers softly weave,
Light dances on the fabric,
Threads of hope we believe.

Each moment a shimmer,
With colors that unite,
In shadows we discover,
The brilliance of the light.

Every heart a lantern,
Radiating pure gold,
Together we find warmth,
In stories yet untold.

From darkness we emerge,
With visions like the dawn,
Each thread a shared journey,
In unity, we're drawn.

With every step we take,
We weave our lives so bright,
A tapestry of souls,
In threads of pure delight.

Awakening in Sync

In the morning's embrace,
Awake with eyes anew,
The world softly whispers,
As nature's song breaks through.

Hearts beating to the rhythm,
In harmony we sway,
Bound by love's gentle pull,
We greet the brand-new day.

Awakening together,
Each moment feels alive,
With every shared heartbeat,
It's here that dreams survive.

In the dance of the cosmos,
We find our place in time,
Awaking in sync,
Our spirits start to climb.

Together we ignite,
The fire deep within,
In the rhythm of our souls,
New journeys now begin.

Flickers of Unity

In a world so divided,
We find sparks in the night,
Flickers of unity shine,
Guiding us to the light.

Through struggles and triumphs,
Our spirits intertwine,
In every moment shared,
Our hearts begin to align.

Though storms may surround us,
And shadows seem to grow,
Together we're stronger,
In love's warm, gentle glow.

Flickers become flames,
As bonds begin to form,
In unity of purpose,
We rise and transform.

The sparks of connection,
Light paths we've yet to tread,
With flickers of unity,
Our journey may be led.

Sunlit Journeys

In the dawn's first light,
Adventures start to bloom,
With each step we wander,
Dispersing all the gloom.

Underneath the vast sky,
We roam where shadows fade,
Sunlit journeys await,
Where dreams will not cascade.

The horizon whispers hopes,
Calling us to explore,
With every ray that shines,
We find what we adore.

Together, hand in hand,
We follow golden beams,
On sunlit journeys shared,
We'll live our wildest dreams.

Through every twist and turn,
In warmth, we stand as one,
Embracing every moment,
Until the day is done.

Celestial Moments

Stars twinkle high in the night,
Whispers of dreams take their flight.
Moonbeams dance on gentle streams,
Embracing the magic of our dreams.

Clouds drift soft in twilight's glow,
Each breath a moment, new to bestow.
Time stands still as we find our way,
In celestial realms where we wish to stay.

A meteor streaks across the vast,
A fleeting glimpse of life unsurpassed.
We search for meaning in the skies,
Finding solace where the universe lies.

Auroras paint the dark with flair,
A symphony of colors, beyond compare.
Nature's canvas, stretched so wide,
Inviting us all to take a ride.

In this expanse where wonders bloom,
We feel the heat, dispelling gloom.
Nestled in cosmic serenity,
Celestial moments set us free.

Bound by Radiance

In the dawn's soft, golden hue,
Hearts entwine in a bond so true.
Radiance flows through every gaze,
Filling our world with warm arrays.

Hands clasped tight beneath the sun,
Together we shine, two as one.
A heartbeat echoing in the light,
Guiding us through day and night.

The glow of love, a lasting flame,
Forever igniting, never the same.
In laughter's echo and softest sighs,
Bound by radiance, time softly flies.

Through stormy skies and gentle rains,
We stand united, despite the pains.
Each trial faced, we rise anew,
A brightness forged in love so true.

As twilight falls, we share a spark,
Two souls igniting against the dark.
Forever we'll shine, a beacon bright,
Bound by radiance, love takes flight.

The Sun's Caress

Morning breaks with gentle grace,
Sunlight spills in a warm embrace.
Fields awaken, kissed by gold,
Nature's secrets beginning to unfold.

Soft winds whisper a sweet refrain,
Carrying remnants of night's soft rain.
Every petal shines with dew,
The world's a canvas, bright and new.

Children laugh beneath the beams,
Chasing shadows, living dreams.
The sun's caress upon their face,
Illuminating joy, a warm embrace.

Time slows down in summer's glow,
Each moment cherished, we let it flow.
Golden hours drift into the past,
Yet with the sun, the love holds fast.

As daylight fades, the sun will dip,
Leaving a mark on each sweet sip.
The promise of warmth in the night,
The sun's caress, our guiding light.

Daylight Dreams

In the dawn's embrace, dreams are sown,
Awakening hearts, never alone.
Chasing shadows of night's retreat,
We find our paths where daylight meets.

Fields of color burst into view,
Imagination soars, bold and true.
Every thought wrapped in golden rays,
Guiding us through our unspoken ways.

Moments linger like clouds above,
Whispers of hope, wrapped in love.
Each heartbeat a rhythm, a gentle stream,
Flowing forth in daylight dreams.

As sunsets glow, our wishes rise,
Painting stories across the skies.
With every star that starts to gleam,
We hold tight to our daylight dreams.

In every glance, in every smile,
Daylight lingers for just a while.
We close our eyes, and with a sigh,
Embrace our dreams as day floats by.

Bonds of the Early Light

In morning's glow, we rise anew,
With whispers soft, the dreams pursue.
The sun breaks forth, a gentle beam,
We weave our hopes, a vibrant theme.

In laughter shared, we find our way,
Each heartbeat counts, through night and day.
With hands entwined, we face the dawn,
United strong, forever drawn.

The shadows fade, as trust takes flight,
In every spark, a shared delight.
Together we stand, side by side,
In bonds of love, we do abide.

Through trials faced, we bravely stand,
In every storm, we understand.
As dawn emerges, bright and clear,
Our hearts unite, we cast out fear.

Embrace the light, let our hearts sing,
In every moment, joy we bring.
The early light, a wondrous sight,
In bonds we forge, our spirits bright.

Burning Embers of Unity

In the heart where fire glows,
Embers spark, as friendship grows.
With every shared, sweet memory,
We light the night with unity.

In whispers soft, our voices blend,
Through every curve, around each bend.
Together strong, we forge our fate,
In laughter loud, we celebrate.

The warmth we share, a sacred trust,
Through trials deep, in love we must.
Each flicker bright, our spirits soar,
Bound by the flame, forevermore.

As shadows fall, our hope ignites,
In darkest hours, we find our lights.
The embers dance, a fiery spree,
Together we stand, in harmony.

In every heart, a spark remains,
Through storms and joy, through losses, gains.
As burning embers, our souls entwined,
In unity's glow, our hearts aligned.

Celestial Dance

Under the stars, we find our way,
The moonlit beams, they softly sway.
In cosmic dreams, we laugh and glide,
In every twirl, we find our pride.

With every step, the galaxies spin,
A rhythm found, where love begins.
In every gaze, the starlight gleams,
Together we chase, the whispered dreams.

The universe sings, a lullaby,
As constellations paint the sky.
In this embrace, our spirits flow,
In each other's arms, we gently grow.

Through cosmic paths, our hearts entwine,
In endless space, your hand in mine.
The dance we share, a timeless trance,
In the realm of stars, we take our chance.

So let the night, our guide, remain,
In every beat, we break the chain.
As we glide through the cosmic sea,
In this celestial dance, we're free.

Daybreak's Harmony

As night slips by, the dawn unfolds,
With colors bright, the day beholds.
In gentle hues, the world awakes,
A melody of joy it makes.

In whispered breezes, secrets shared,
With every breath, our souls laid bare.
In harmony, we find our ground,
In every note, life's beauty found.

The sun ascends, a golden grace,
We chase the light, a warm embrace.
With every step, in sync we tread,
In daybreak's heart, our paths are led.

Together we sing, a hopeful tune,
In every rise, beneath the moon.
As day unfolds, our spirits soar,
In daybreak's harmony, we explore.

Through hills and valleys, boundless wide,
In nature's song, we will abide.
With every dawn, a fresh start given,
In daybreak's light, our souls are risen.

Celestial Symphony of Us

Under the stars, we dance in the night,
A melody woven, our spirits take flight.
Whispers of starlight, soft and divine,
Together we bask, in the warmth of the shine.

The moon sings of secrets, of dreams intertwined,
In this cosmic embrace, our hearts unconfined.
Galaxies twinkle, they echo our song,
In this celestial ballet, we both belong.

Crickets are chirping, a harmonious tune,
As shadows delight in the glow of the moon.
We share whispered stories, the past and the new,
In the silence of night, it's just me and you.

Each star holds a promise, each wish draws us near,
In this symphony cosmic, I feel you right here.
With soft breaths and laughter, we compose our refrain,
This heavenly journey is ours to sustain.

As dawn starts to break, painting skies in gold,
Our love's everlasting, a tale to be told.
In the celestial dance, let's forever stay,
A symphony written, in stardust we play.

Fading Night's Embrace

The shadows grow long as the sun starts to rise,
In the fading night's embrace, we bid our goodbyes.
Whispers of twilight still linger around,
In the stillness of dusk, love's echoes abound.

Stars twinkle faintly, as dreams start to flee,
The cool breeze reminds me how fleeting we be.
Flickering candles cast shadows on walls,
As night's gentle presence begins to withdraw.

Yet in this transition from dark into light,
The magic of memories shines ever so bright.
For every end signifies a new dawn,
In the dance of the moments, our spirits are drawn.

With each breath of morning, let go of the night,
Embrace what's ahead, let the sunlight ignite.
While fading night's whispers may soon disappear,
The echoes of our hearts will always be near.

So cherish the twilight, the beauty it brings,
In the warmth of the daylight, our love softly sings.
For even in parting, a promise remains,
In the fading night's song, true love never wanes.

Tapestry of the Eventide

Threads of twilight weave through the sky,
In hues of lavender, where daywaves die.
Crimson and orange paint each gentle breath,
A tapestry glowing, defying all death.

The lengthening shadows stretch across the land,
As the sun bows gracefully, hand in hand.
Each stitch tells a story, a moment in time,
In this fabric of dusk, our lives softly rhyme.

The whispers of evening bring peace to the soul,
As stars begin twinkling, their soft, silver shoal.
The universe wraps us in gentle embrace,
In the tapestry woven, we find our own place.

Dreams float like feathers, carried on high,
In this magical hour, the spirit can fly.
While night covers gently, our worries subside,
Together we create, as the world turns its tide.

So hold tight the moments; let time gently fade,
In the tapestry of dusk, memories are made.
Each thread weaves an echo, a heartbeat, a sigh,
In this ever-changing sky, love learns to fly.

The Spark of New Beginnings

In the hush of the dawn, a new chapter starts,
With hopes painted bright on each eager heart.
The whispers of promise in the morning air,
Ignite in our souls, a vision so rare.

A flicker of courage breaks through the night,
In the warmth of the sun, we stand in the light.
Each sunrise a canvas, each moment a chance,
To dance with our dreams in a passionate trance.

With every small step, we take on the path,
Embracing the journey, its joy and its wrath.
For the spark of new beginnings is yours and is mine,
A beacon of hope, where our lives intertwine.

Let go of tomorrow, the past's heavy weight,
In this sacred sunrise, let love dictate.
With laughter and kindness, we'll cultivate dreams,
In the garden of life, where possibility beams.

So rise with the sun, let your spirits ascend,
In the magic of mornings, all doubts meet their end.
For new beginnings await with a wink and a jest,
In this dance of our lives, we are truly blessed.

Hearts Illuminated by Dawn's Kiss

Sunlight creeps over hills,
Awakening the silent dreams.
Whispers of a heart that thrills,
In the glow of golden beams.

Softly paints the world anew,
Colors dancing in the air.
Every moment feels so true,
Lost in hues beyond compare.

Chasing shadows of the night,
Fading gently with the dawn.
Hearts are filled with pure delight,
As the dark is swiftly gone.

Nature's symphony begins,
Birds rejoice in early flight.
With each note, the spirit wins,
Welcoming the day so bright.

Together souls ignite the flame,
In this radiant morning light.
Dreams awakened, none the same,
Hearts illuminated, take flight.

Rising Forth in Shared Light.

Two souls meet beneath the sun,
Kindred spirits, side by side.
In this journey, we are one,
Thriving where our hopes abide.

With every step beneath the sky,
Hand in hand, we face the day.
In your gaze, I find my why,
Together, we will find our way.

Mountains rise, and rivers flow,
Together, we will forge our path.
Facing storms, we'll ebb and flow,
Finding joy within the wrath.

In the warmth of morning's grace,
Hearts entwined, we'll dance along.
Every smile upon our face,
Echoing a shared love song.

With our dreams, we'll light the way,
Rising forth in love's embrace.
Brighter with each passing day,
In this journey, we find our place.

Morning's Embrace

Awakening in soft embrace,
Sunlight drapes the world in gold.
Gentle warmth, a tender face,
Promises of stories told.

Whispers carried by the breeze,
Rustling leaves in morning's light.
Nature's symphony will please,
As daybreak conquers fleeting night.

In the stillness, peace cascades,
Calming hearts and lifting souls.
Each moment, magic invades,
Morning's touch makes us feel whole.

With the dawn, our fears subside,
Hope is cradled in the air.
In this light, we find our guide,
United in a love so rare.

Every heartbeat sings a song,
In this peace, we belong here.
Together, we will journey long,
In morning's embrace, there's no fear.

Dawn's Tapestry

Threads of light weave through the trees,
Golden strands of sunlit hue.
Nature's quilt, a work of ease,
Each stitch tells a tale so true.

Birds take flight in morning's air,
Colors splash against the sky.
In this moment free from care,
We let our spirits soar and fly.

With each ray, new dreams unfold,
Painting visions in our hearts.
Stories whispered, bright and bold,
As the day and night depart.

Softly gliding on the breeze,
Dawn invites us to explore.
In this world, we find our keys,
Unlocking treasures and much more.

Embrace the dawn, let worries fade,
In this tapestry of light.
Hand in hand, the journey made,
Together, we will chase the bright.

Brightening Paths

Through the woods, the sunlight beams,
Painting gold on gentle streams.
Each step forward, a dance of light,
Guiding souls with hopes in sight.

Whispers of nature softly call,
Echoing dreams, lest we fall.
Every shadow, a story told,
In the warmth, our hearts unfold.

Blossoms sway in vibrant hues,
Offering courage to those who choose.
On this journey, hand in hand,
Together forging a brighter land.

The road ahead, unknown and wide,
But with each other, we will bide.
Shining moments, bit by bit,
Creating paths where friendships knit.

Let the stars above us shine,
A map of wishes that align.
In the embrace of twilight's kiss,
Find the magic in simple bliss.

Together in Radiance

In the glow of twilight's grace,
We find solace in this place.
Hand in hand, our dreams ignite,
Together, we embrace the night.

The moonlight dances on our skin,
Each heartbeat a familiar hymn.
With laughter shared, we light the dark,
Together, forever, we leave our mark.

In every shadow, a story shines,
Eternal love in subtle signs.
Wrapped in warmth, we breathe as one,
Chasing the dreams until they're spun.

Stars above, our guiding lights,
Filling our hearts, igniting flights.
In radiant moments, we unfold,
An everlasting tale retold.

Together we shall brave the storm,
Our spirits intertwined and warm.
With every glance, our hopes ascend,
In this journey, love will never end.

A New Day's Promise

Morning breaks, a gentle sigh,
Awakening dreams that touch the sky.
With the sun, a fresh start glows,
In every heart, new potential grows.

Birds serenade the dawn's embrace,
A melody of hope, a sacred space.
In the stillness, a chance to rise,
To paint the world in brighter skies.

With each sunrise, we dare to dream,
Finding strength in every seam.
Through the struggles, we will find,
A new day's promise in our mind.

Moments linger, soft and bright,
Guiding us through the endless night.
Every heartbeat marks the start,
Of journeys woven with hope and heart.

Let the colors of life unfold,
A tapestry of stories told.
In every whisper, a lovely way,
To cherish the gift of a new day.

Mornings Entwined

As dawn unfurls her golden hue,
Awakening dreams in morning's brew.
Together we greet the day anew,
With open hearts and skies so blue.

The gentle breeze, a calming song,
Reminding us where we belong.
In the warmth of sun-kissed rays,
Our worries erased in morning's blaze.

With laughter dancing on the air,
Every moment precious and rare.
Mornings painted in brush strokes bright,
Entwined in love, we face the light.

Fields of flowers, colors rise,
In harmony with our shared sighs.
Stretching wide, our hopes align,
In this canvas, our lives entwine.

As the day unfolds with grace,
We find joy in each other's space.
In the tapestry of love we twine,
Mornings shine, forever divine.

Rise and Shine

Awake anew with morning's grace,
The sun peeks through, a warm embrace.
Nature sings a joyful tune,
Brighten hearts with golden bloom.

Birds take flight across the sky,
Chasing dreams as they soar high.
Waves of light, a gentle breeze,
Whispers hope among the trees.

Each moment holds a chance to start,
A canvas clean, a beating heart.
Embrace the day, let worries cease,
In every step, discover peace.

So rise and shine, let shadows flee,
Unfold your spirit, wild and free.
With eyes wide open, take the chance,
Join the world's enchanting dance.

Beams of Connection

In the night, the stars align,
Guiding souls through paths divine.
Each tiny light, a tale to share,
Weaving bonds that linger in air.

Hands entwined in silent trust,
Moments cherished, memories rust.
Bridges built on whispered dreams,
Flowing freely like gentle streams.

Laughter echoes in the dark,
Every smile ignites a spark.
Unified in joy and pain,
Together we rise, together we gain.

Though distance may stretch far and wide,
In hearts we hold the strongest tide.
With every heartbeat, we'll remind,
In love's embrace, we're intertwined.

Unfolding Horizons

Horizons stretch beyond the view,
Colors blend in every hue.
Step by step, we venture forth,
Seeking treasures of the earth.

Mountains rise and valleys call,
Paths to wander, dreams to install.
Beneath the sky, our spirits rise,
With hopeful hearts, we claim the prize.

Each dawn whispers, 'Take the leap,'
Into the unknown, where secrets sleep.
Winds will guide you, trust the flow,
In the journey, let your heart glow.

With open minds, explore the vast,
Embrace the present, learn from past.
In every challenge, find the light,
Unfolding horizons, bold and bright.

Reflections in Light

In still waters, dreams reside,
Ripples whisper from deep inside.
Shimmering hopes dance in the sun,
Moments captured, life's race run.

Through the glass, the world unfolds,
Stories of warmth, tales retold.
Each glimmer shines a truth so bright,
Guiding lost souls through the night.

In shadows cast, we search for grace,
Finding beauty in every space.
Reflections tell what words may hide,
A tapestry woven, life's great guide.

So pause and gaze upon the flow,
In light's embrace, let feelings grow.
For in each glance, a world resides,
Reflections in light, where love abides.

Twilight Whispers

The sun dips low in the sky,
Whispers of night softly sigh.
Stars begin to blink and gleam,
In the dusk, we find our dream.

Shadows dance on the cool ground,
Magic in silence, profound.
A soft breeze carries our tune,
Crickets sing beneath the moon.

Colors fade, but hearts ignite,
In twilight's embrace, all feels right.
Hope lingers in the pale light,
As we hold the coming night.

Lost in thoughts of the day past,
Moments cherished, memories cast.
In the glow of the evening's brace,
Together, we find our space.

The world slows down, time stands still,
In this magic, we get our fill.
Twilight whispers, secrets unfold,
A story of love quietly told.

Seasons of Togetherness

In spring's bloom, our laughter rings,
Flowers dance with the joy life brings.
Sunshine warms our tender hearts,
In this season, togetherness starts.

Summer days bathe us in gold,
Memories made, cherished and bold.
With every sunset, love grows bright,
A canvas painted with pure delight.

Autumn leaves fall like soft rain,
Colors burst, yet shadows remain.
Hand in hand, through this change we roam,
In shifting tides, we find our home.

Winter's chill wraps us so tight,
Under blankets, hearts ignite.
With each snowfall, dreams arise,
In the quiet, love never dies.

Through each season, we intertwine,
In every moment, you are mine.
Together, we weather the storm,
In love's embrace, we are reborn.

Embracing Day's Birth

Morning breaks with softest light,
Birds awaken, take their flight.
The world stirs from slumber deep,
In this moment, dreams we keep.

The sky blushes with hues of gold,
Whispers of stories yet untold.
With each ray, hope fills the air,
A promise made, forever fair.

As the sun climbs, shadows wane,
Nature sings a sweet refrain.
Deeper breaths and open hearts,
In each sunrise, a brand new start.

Together, we rise with the dawn,
In this dance, our fears are gone.
With warm embraces, hand in hand,
In the light, we boldly stand.

The day unfolds, bright and new,
A canvas waiting, just for two.
Embracing all that life will bring,
In unity, our spirits sing.

Kaleidoscope of Us

In every moment, colors blend,
A vibrant world, around the bend.
Through shifting patterns, we explore,
A kaleidoscope that ever soars.

With laughter bright, and eyes that shine,
Every fragment tells a line.
Reflections of the love we share,
In this journey, free and rare.

Twists and turns, a wondrous flow,
Through ups and downs, we always grow.
In each hue, a story told,
Chasing dreams, both brave and bold.

When shadows loom, we create light,
Filling pathways, hearts ignite.
Together, we paint the skies above,
A masterpiece woven from love.

In the mosaic of our days,
Every glance, a gentle praise.
Kaleidoscope of you and me,
A symphony of harmony.

Kaleidoscope of First Light

Morning breezes softly play,
Colors burst to greet the day.
Whispers dance on golden beams,
Nature wakes from night's sweet dreams.

Petals shimmer, dew drops gleam,
Sunlight flows like a warm stream.
Bird songs weave in the bright air,
Joyful moments everywhere.

Shadows fade, the world ignites,
Painting skies with pure delights.
In this dawn, a promise made,
Beauty thrives in light displayed.

Glimmers touch each vibrant scene,
A dazzling tapestry unseen.
Each color speaks, a sigh, a cheer,
In this kaleidoscope, we steer.

Every heartbeat, every sigh,
Caught in the vast and waking sky.
Life unfolds in hues so bold,
As the story of dawn is told.

Becoming One with the Dawn

As night retreats, the cosmos sighs,
A canvas bright, where silence lies.
Golden rays reach out to touch,
In this moment, we feel so much.

Breath of morn brings calm and peace,
Nature's whispers never cease.
Embracing light, we shed the night,
In quiet harmony, we feel right.

Clouds drift softly, dreams unfold,
Stories of the earth retold.
With each ray, our spirits rise,
Lost in wonder, we touch the skies.

A gentle warmth wraps us tight,
Cradled in morning's tender light.
As shadows fade, our fears subside,
We become one, with love as guide.

In the dawn's embrace, we stand,
Hearts united, hand in hand.
Each moment shines, a fleeting spark,
Together bright, we'll leave a mark.

Harmony of the Celestial Skies

Stars align in tranquil dance,
Celestial whispers, a cosmic chance.
Moonbeams cradle the earth below,
In tranquil night, our spirits glow.

Galaxies spin, a jeweled art,
Bringing peace to every heart.
In the stillness, dreams take flight,
Captured in the velvet night.

Meteor trails blaze across the dark,
Wishes made on every spark.
Constellations tell their lore,
Binding souls forevermore.

As the night cradles our fears,
Laughter echoes, soft as tears.
Underneath the cosmic dome,
We find solace, we find home.

Harmony sings in quiet grace,
Each heartbeat finds its rightful place.
In this unity, we brightly thrive,
In the celestial dance, we come alive.

Illuminated Journeys

Footsteps trace the path of light,
Guiding us through endless night.
Every journey, a story told,
In the glow, our dreams unfold.

Through the mist, we find our way,
Chasing shadows, welcoming day.
With each step, we learn to roam,
In this journey, we find home.

Mountains rise, valleys call,
In every stumble, we grow tall.
Paths may twist, the road may bend,
But light will shine around the bend.

Voices echo, soft and clear,
Sharing tales of love and fear.
In the warmth of shared delight,
We illuminate the darkest night.

Every traveler holds a spark,
Shining bright, igniting the dark.
Together, we roam through time and space,
On illuminated journeys, we find grace.

Whispers of the Dawn

In the hush of morning light,
Softly whispers come to play.
Birds begin their sweet delight,
Chasing night's last shades away.

As the world awakens slow,
Colors bloom in gentle grace.
Winds of change begin to blow,
Painting dreams on nature's face.

With each breath, the day unfolds,
Promises of hope anew.
Gentle stories waiting told,
In the sky's vast ocean blue.

Sunrise paints the empty skies,
Gold and amber, fiery hues.
Nature lifts its sleepy eyes,
As the dawn begins to muse.

Every shadow takes its flight,
Wrapped in warm and tender beams.
In the whispers of the night,
Linger still the fading dreams.

Embrace of the First Light

Morning breaks with softest glow,
Nature wakes from silent night.
In the air, a magic flow,
Welcoming the first sweet light.

Mountains kissed by golden rays,
Fields awaken, dew in sight.
Every creature finds its ways,
In the cradle of daylight.

Gentle whispers fill the air,
Promises of warmth unfold.
Every moment, free from care,
In the hands of morning's hold.

Sunrise dances on the leaves,
Casting shadows, soft and bright.
In its arms, the dream believes,
Lost forever in pure delight.

This embrace, a tender start,
Filling souls with endless cheer.
As the day plays out its part,
Every heartbeat draws it near.

The Colors Between Us

In the twilight, we find grace,
Painted skies of rich design.
Every hue a warm embrace,
Courage blooms as hearts align.

Violet whispers, azure dreams,
Brush the canvas of the day.
In our eyes, the longing beams,
Coloring the words we say.

Blues and greens in harmony,
Swaying gently with the breeze.
Together, we feel so free,
Lost in nature's tender tease.

Sunset's palette, bold and bright,
Strokes of orange, crimson fire.
Every shadow holds the light,
Colors spark our hearts' desire.

As the night's curtain descends,
Stars in violets and in cream.
With each moment, the heart mends,
In the colors of our dream.

Chasing Morning's Glow

In the dawn's sweet silent call,
Chasing dreams on sparkling dew.
Rays of light begin to fall,
Painting visions fresh and new.

In the garden where we roam,
Every petal breathes the day.
Finding solace, we call home,
In the light where shadows play.

Gentle whispers of the breeze,
Float like notes of morning songs.
Nature bends upon its knees,
To the glow where hope belongs.

With each step, our spirits rise,
Chasing light with pure intent.
In the warmth that softly ties,
Threads of joy that life presents.

As the sun breaks through the gray,
Painting us in golden streaks,
We embrace the bright array,
In this dance, our hearts do speak.

Illuminated Lives

In shadows deep, we find our way,
Each spark ignites, a bright display.
Together we rise, hand in hand,
Illuminated by dreams unplanned.

A beacon shines, a guiding light,
Through darkest nights, we chase the bright.
With hearts ablaze, we leave the past,
In this embrace, we are steadfast.

Every story holds a flame,
In whispered hopes, we share the name.
Voices blend in harmonic tone,
As we dance through the unknown.

With every step, our spirits soar,
Through trials faced, we ask for more.
United we stand, no more alone,
In this journey, we've truly grown.

As stars align, our paths are clear,
With love as guide, we conquer fear.
Illuminated lives, we share the way,
In this kaleidoscope, we choose to stay.

Rising Together

When dawn breaks soft, we lift our eyes,
With hope anew, we touch the skies.
In harmony, our voices blend,
As hearts unite, the wounds will mend.

Through stormy weather, side by side,
Together strong, we'll turn the tide.
With courage deep, we'll face the fight,
In every shadow, we find the light.

In dreams entwined, we pave a way,
With every step, we choose to stay.
A brighter path, we weave with care,
For every soul, a bond we share.

With laughter ringing, joy takes flight,
In passion's fire, we burn so bright.
Together rising, hand in hand,
A tapestry of love so grand.

As mountains high we dare to scale,
In unity, we shall prevail.
Through every trial, our spirits soar,
Together rising, forevermore.

Tides of Unity

The ocean's waves, they ebb and flow,
In every tide, a chance to grow.
With hearts as one, we stand so tall,
In unity, together, we call.

Whispers of the sea, they resonate,
A melody of fate we celebrate.
With open arms, we greet the day,
In every moment, we find our way.

Through storms and calm, we intertwine,
In currents strong, our souls align.
With every heartbeat, a rhythm shared,
In these tides of love, we are prepared.

From distant shores, we find our place,
With every step, a warm embrace.
In every wave, a story told,
In unity's grace, our hearts unfold.

As sun sets low, and stars appear,
We'll ride the tides, dismiss our fear.
In this vast sea, we find our truth,
In tides of unity, eternal youth.

Daybreak's Reunion

When sunrise greets the morning haze,
We find our paths in gentle blaze.
In warmth of dawn, we come alive,
Together now, we thrive and strive.

With colors bright, we paint the sky,
In collaboration, we cannot lie.
Through whispered dreams, we touch the heart,
In every beat, we play our part.

As shadows fade, the light unfolds,
In every story, a truth retold.
With hands held tight, we walk the line,
In daybreak's glow, our souls combine.

The moments shared, like scattered seeds,
In fertile ground, they sprout from needs.
In unity, we craft our fate,
With every sunrise, we create.

As day unfolds, our spirits rise,
In hearts of gold, we claim the prize.
Through daybreak's reunion, we find our way,
In every moment, come what may.

Silhouettes at Sunrise

In the morning's gentle glow,
Shadows dance upon the land.
Whispers of the night still flow,
As daybreak takes its stand.

Ghostly forms embrace the light,
Sketches of a world reborn.
Colors burst, dispelling night,
Hope is woven, dreams adorned.

Birds take flight in vibrant skies,
Echoes of a brand new day.
Nature's chorus softly sighs,
In unison, they play.

Time unwinds its endless thread,
Painting moments, pure and bright.
With each heartbeat, fears are shed,
As dawn unveils its might.

In this magic, time shall freeze,
Moments stitched in golden hues.
Silhouettes sway in the breeze,
A canvas bright, dreams to choose.

Illuminated Pathways

Beneath the moon's soft silver light,
Paths twinkle like distant stars.
Each step taken feels so right,
Erasing all of yesterday's scars.

Whispers echo from the trees,
Guiding hearts where shadows dwell.
Nature's breathing, like a breeze,
Carries stories only time can tell.

Every turn, a new delight,
Glimmers spark in hidden nooks.
The night holds secrets, shining bright,
Inviting souls to read the books.

With every step a choice is made,
To wander deep or stay in light.
In this journey, fears will fade,
As we chase the dreams in flight.

Together over paths we glide,
Friends and kin, a faithful band.
Illuminated, side by side,
We write our stories, hand in hand.

Radiant Bonds

Threads of light weave through the air,
Connections spark with every glance.
Moments shared, a silent prayer,
To love, to trust, we take a chance.

In laughter's glow, we find our way,
Hearts united, fierce and strong.
Through the storm or sunny day,
In harmony, we sing our song.

Ties that bind, so deeply sewn,
Our spirits dance, entwined in fate.
Through life's trials, we've grown,
Together, we shall resonate.

With every hug, each whispered word,
A flame ignites, forever bright.
In shared silence, love is heard,
As shadows fade, embracing light.

Radiant bonds we do embrace,
Filling spaces with pure love.
In this journey, safe in grace,
Together, we rise high above.

The Dawn's Promise

Awakening beneath the sky,
The glow of dawn begins to bloom.
Fleeting dreams begin to fly,
Illuminating each dark room.

With every ray that graces land,
Hope unfurls its tender wings.
A new day beckons, quietly planned,
Whispers of joy that the sunrise brings.

Life's canvas fresh, waits to be filled,
Colors splash with each heartbeat.
In the dawn, aspirations thrilled,
Adventures beckon, bittersweet.

Promises wrapped in morning light,
Encouraging hearts to embrace.
With a story awaiting our flight,
Life encourages dreams to chase.

As day unfolds, let's tread with grace,
The dawn ignites that sacred spark.
In every journey, find your place,
The promise shines, guiding in the dark.

Colors of Companionship

In laughter's hue, we dance and play,
Friendship's brush paints night and day.
Every shared secret, every cheer,
A palette rich, we hold so dear.

Through storms we stand, side by side,
In the vibrant blend, we take pride.
With colors bright, our bond we weave,
In this masterpiece, we believe.

With every shade, a memory grows,
In the fabric of trust that forever flows.
Woven in joy, and stitched with care,
Together, a canvas beyond compare.

In twilight's glow, a painted sky,
Echoes of laughter that never die.
Sharing our dreams in every hue,
Together, creating a world anew.

In the gallery of life, we stand tall,
A vibrant testament, for one and all.
With colors of love, we fill the space,
In companionship's art, we find our place.

A Tapestry of Dawn

The sun peeks through a misty veil,
Awakening dreams where whispers sail.
Threads of gold in morning's light,
Weaving hopes that take to flight.

With every strand, a story spun,
Of battles fought, of victories won.
In this tapestry of warmth and grace,
Together we find our sacred space.

As colors blend in soft embrace,
New beginnings we dare to trace.
Every dawn, a canvas bare,
With threads of love we choose to share.

Nature sings a symphony bright,
In the hush of dawn's first light.
With vibrant hues, our hearts unite,
In this woven dream, we take flight.

We gather each moment in joyful thread,
In this tapestry, we've bravely tread.
With every dawn, a chance to start,
A portrait of love etched in our heart.

Celestial Whispers

Stars twinkle in the velvet night,
Whispers of dreams taking flight.
Galaxies dance in cosmic grace,
In the quietude, we find our place.

Moonlight kisses the trees below,
Softly guiding where we go.
In the hush of night, our hearts ignite,
Celestial whispers, pure delight.

Each star a wish, each comet a chance,
In this universe, we dare to dance.
With every sigh, the cosmos sighs,
In the magic of night, our spirits rise.

Nebulae bloom in colors true,
Painting skies with every hue.
In the stillness, our secrets gleam,
Beneath the stars, we chase the dream.

With the dawn, these echoes remain,
In the silence, we'll meet again.
As celestial whispers softly fade,
In the heart of night, our bond is made.

The Collective Dawn

As dawn breaks with a golden hue,
Together, we step into the new.
With shared breaths and hearts aligned,
The collective pulse, beautifully entwined.

In unison, we face the day,
Guided by hope in every way.
With laughter rising, fears erased,
In this moment, our dreams are traced.

Together we rise like flowers in spring,
In vibrant hues, our voices sing.
With every challenge, hand in hand,
We build a world that's truly grand.

In the light of dawn, we reflect,
In every smile, a bond perfect.
With hearts as one, we pave the way,
For brighter tomorrows that brightly play.

As the sun climbs high in the azure sky,
With our dreams soaring, we'll never shy.
In this collective dawn, we'll stand tall,
Together, forever, through it all.

Golden Horizons Ahead

In the dawn's gentle glow,
Dreams take flight, we will go.
Chasing shadows of the past,
With hope, our sails are cast.

Golden rays on the sea,
Whispers of what could be.
Every wave, a new chance,
In this bright, endless dance.

Horizons stretch far and wide,
With courage, we'll abide.
Through storms, we'll find our way,
Together, come what may.

Embrace the warmth of dawn,
As darkness slowly is drawn.
Together we forge the light,
In unity, we ignite.

With every step, we collide,
In dreams we will abide.
Golden futures in our sight,
We rise, embracing the light.

Rising Together in Radiance

In the morning's gentle grace,
We find joy in every place.
Hearts aflame, spirits free,
Together we rise, you and me.

Fingers laced in morning's cheer,
Our laughter chasing shadows near.
Hand in hand, we boldly stand,
United in this vibrant land.

With every thought, we create,
A world bright, there's no debate.
Linking dreams, oh so bright,
Together, we'll embrace the light.

As sunbeams paint the skies,
In each moment, our love lies.
Rising high, fierce and strong,
Together, we always belong.

Through trials, our souls combine,
In each other, we brightly shine.
In radiance, we find our bliss,
Together, we rise, sealed with a kiss.

Mornings Woven with Light

Each morning, a canvas pure,
Brushed with hues that may endure.
Gentle beams of golden sun,
Whispering that day's begun.

Birdsong dances on the breeze,
Nature's chorus, hearts at ease.
Woven threads of hope and cheer,
In this moment, we draw near.

Through dewdrops, dreams reflect,
Promises that we connect.
In the light, we find our way,
Mornings bloom, new thoughts array.

With each ray that breaks the dawn,
Shadows fade, and fears are gone.
In the warmth of morning's grace,
We discover our sacred space.

Together, we rise and shine,
Woven with love, pure, divine.
Mornings gifted, spirits bright,
In this world, we share our light.

The Light We Share

In the depths of night's embrace,
We find comfort in this place.
Together, hearts beat as one,
In the dark, we see the sun.

Every whisper forms a spark,
Illuminating paths in dark.
With our hands, we build a flame,
United, we'll never be the same.

Through the storms, we carry on,
With each dawn, new dreams are drawn.
Our souls intertwine so bright,
In connection, we find our light.

With every challenge that we face,
Love's warm glow, our saving grace.
In the shadows, we stand tall,
The light we share, it conquers all.

Together, we'll weave a tale,
In every heartbeat, love prevails.
With courage, together we stand,
The light we share, hand in hand.

Chasing Celestial Light

In the twilight glow, we dance free,
Chasing shadows of the deep blue sea.
Stars whisper secrets from far above,
Guiding our hearts, igniting our love.

With every step, the cosmos in sight,
We soar on dreams, embracing the night.
Celestial beams cast a golden hue,
Every breath speaks of me and of you.

Across the heavens, we revel and glide,
In a universe vast, our spirits abide.
Shooting stars scatter wishes so bright,
Together we wander, chasing the light.

Reflections of Togetherness

In the quiet moments, we find our way,
Echoes of laughter fill the day.
Hands intertwined, as we pause and reflect,
In each other's eyes, love we detect.

Through storms and sunshine, side by side,
We build our dreams, with hearts open wide.
Whispers of comfort in gentle embrace,
Together we flourish, in love's endless space.

With every heartbeat, our memories grow,
A tapestry woven, with threads we sow.
In the canvas of life, our colors unite,
Painting the world with our radiant light.

Vibrant Touches

In the garden, colors bloom and sway,
Petals unfurl, greeting the day.
With each gentle brush, our senses ignite,
Inspired by beauty, pure and delight.

Fingers like melodies dance through the air,
Creating connections, tender and rare.
A vibrant palette of feelings and dreams,
Painting emotions, bursting at seams.

Sunrise kisses the earth, soft and warm,
We mingle with nature, lost in its charm.
Every touch sings of stories untold,
In the symphony of life, we uphold.

Echoes of Morning

With dawn's first light, a new day begins,
Whispers of hope ride the gentle winds.
Birds serenade the sky with their song,
As the world awakens, where we belong.

Golden rays stretch through the trees,
Carrying warmth in the softest breeze.
Each breath we take is drenched in delight,
Echoes of morning, pure and bright.

In the quiet moments, we find our peace,
As dreams take flight, and worries cease.
Every heartbeat syncs with nature's embrace,
In the echoes of morning, we find our place.

Reflections in the Daybreak

Morning whispers softly,
New light graces the ground.
Dreams of night now fading,
Hope is where we're bound.

A river of golden hue,
Flows beneath the trees.
Petals open to the sky,
Swaying with the breeze.

Shadows retreat slowly,
As warmth begins to rise.
Nature hums a sweet tune,
Underneath brightening skies.

With each new dawn we find,
Promises held so near.
Reflecting on the past,
Embracing all we hear.

In this tranquil moment,
Time stands still and true.
Daybreak gifts us solace,
In every shade and hue.

Solstice of Healing Hearts

Gathered in a circle,
A warmth that we impart.
Hands entwined like branches,
Connected, soul to heart.

The sun stands still above,
A pause in the great run.
In the light, we find peace,
Together, we are one.

Each story a gemstone,
In the fabric of our own.
Sharing laughter and tears,
No longer alone.

Breath of life surrounds us,
With every word we share.
As seasons start to change,
We rise, we learn, we care.

From the ashes of sadness,
New blooms begin to show.
In the solstice of healing,
Love's soft, gentle glow.

As Light Breaks Over Us

Gentle rays of morning,
Brush away the night.
Embracing every shadow,
Bringing forth the light.

The horizon blushes red,
With promise in its wake.
A symphony of colors,
For our spirits' sake.

Hope springs from the darkness,
A fountain of pure joy.
With each new dawn unfolding,
We find what none destroy.

As light breaks over us,
New dreams begin to soar.
Unfurling with the sunrise,
Opening each door.

Together in the warmth,
We step into the day.
Hand in hand we wander,
Chasing clouds away.

Stars Yielding to Sunbeams

Stars begin to tremble,
Fading from our view.
As the sun awakens,
Brightening skies anew.

Dreams whispered in silence,
Now echo in the day.
With every beam of sunlight,
A promise lights the way.

Galaxies of memories,
We hold them oh so dear.
In the balance of the night,
And day that draws us near.

Hope cascades like sunlight,
Illuminating souls.
Stars yield to the sunbeams,
Fulfilling all our goals.

In the dance of daybreak,
We find a path so clear.
With stars that fade to whispers,
Bright futures now appear.

Collective Heartbeat

In the rhythm, we find our place,
With hearts entwined, we feel the grace.
Every pulse, a song we share,
In harmony, we breathe the air.

Voices merge, a vibrant song,
In unity, where we belong.
Together strong, we rise and soar,
A collective heart forevermore.

In silence, whispers catch the light,
Each beat echoes through the night.
Bound by dreams, we dare to chase,
With every heartbeat, we embrace.

Through trials faced, our spirits bind,
In every loss, new strength we find.
Together we stand, fierce and proud,
A heartbeat shared amid the crowd.

And in that pulse, a legacy,
A tapestry of you and me.
Together here, forever strong,
In love's embrace, we all belong.

When Day Breaks

With dawn's first light, the shadows fade,
A canvas bright, new hopes are laid.
Each ray a promise, warm and sweet,
In morning's glow, our hearts compete.

Birds take flight, the world awakes,
Soft whispers of all it takes.
In colors bold, dreams ignite,
When day breaks forth, we take to flight.

The sun ascends, igniting flames,
To chase away the night's cold claims.
With each new hour, beginnings bloom,
In every heart, dispelling gloom.

Time wanders on, yet so serene,
A dance of light on silken green.
In every moment, find your place,
When day breaks through, feel the embrace.

And as the dusk begins to fall,
Remember light embraces all.
With every dawn, let spirits rise,
When day breaks, we touch the skies.

United in Light

In every spark, a world unfolds,
Each story shared is worth its gold.
Together we shine, a dazzling sight,
Hand in hand, united in light.

Through tangled paths and winding ways,
We illuminate the darkest days.
In every heart, a flicker glows,
A beacon bright, our courage shows.

With shared laughter, we break the night,
Creating warmth, a boundless flight.
Together we reach, grasping the stars,
United always, despite our scars.

In whispered dreams, our spirits soar,
Through ups and downs, we ask for more.
A tapestry woven from love's thread,
United in light, where hope is bred.

With open hearts, we find our place,
In every shadow, we leave a trace.
Together we journey, our spirits bright,
Forever bound, united in light.

Spectrum of Souls

In every hue, a story lies,
A spectrum drawn across the skies.
In colors bright, we find our voice,
A chorus rich, we all rejoice.

Through varying shades, we learn to see,
The beauty found in you and me.
Each heart a shade, each soul a spark,
Together weaving light from dark.

In gentle whispers, we find our way,
With every color, a new display.
A vivid dance, where spirits blend,
In this spectrum, love transcends.

As seasons shift, our colors change,
Embracing growth, we rearrange.
In every smile, a vivid glow,
The spectrum of souls continues to grow.

With all our shades, we paint the world,
A masterpiece in love unfurled.
Together here, our hearts console,
In every shade, we are made whole.

Bridging Horizons

Across the waters, dreams align,
A path unfolds, both yours and mine.
Together we stand, hand in hand,
Building bridges, a future so grand.

Mountains may rise, valleys may fall,
With every step, we heed the call.
Beyond the limits, we shall roam,
Finding solace, in the unknown.

Threads of hope weave through the air,
In unity, nothing we bear.
The sun sets low, yet hearts ignite,
Chasing horizons, chasing the light.

Whispers of courage in twilight glow,
Together we conquer, together we grow.
Visions merging, colors combine,
Creating a tapestry, yours and mine.

As twilight fades to starlit skies,
In every shadow, bright truth lies.
So we journey, with dreams to share,
Bridging horizons, with love and care.

Lightwaves of Togetherness

In the morning, a dance begins,
Lightwaves flicker, warmth within.
Hearts embrace, in friendship's glow,
Together we rise, together we flow.

Through the laughter, shadows fade,
In shared moments, memories are made.
Soft whispers echo under the sun,
In unity's light, we're never done.

A river of dreams flows side by side,
With each heartbeat, love will abide.
Clouds may gather, storms may rage,
But together we turn a new page.

In radiant colors, our spirits soar,
Breaking barriers, opening doors.
With every step, our futures blend,
Lightwaves of togetherness never end.

Under starlit skies, we hold the night,
Infinitesimal echoes of pure delight.
Together we shimmer, together we gleam,
In harmony's rhythm, we are the dream.

Shared Skies

Beneath the vast and endless blue,
We share dreams only we knew.
Clouds drift gently, painting the air,
In every sigh, love's light we share.

A tapestry woven from laughter and tears,
Carried by hope, the heart steers.
As stars twinkle in the twilight's embrace,
We find our solace, our sacred space.

With whispers of wind, old tales we tell,
In the silence of night, where wishes dwell.
United in shadows, forever we stand,
Hand in hand, through this beautiful land.

Under the moon, our spirits unite,
Guided by dreams that take flight.
Together we wander, minds open wide,
In awe of the world, no need to hide.

Days may pass, seasons will change,
But our bond remains, never to rearrange.
In the vastness, we find our ties,
Together as one, beneath shared skies.

Reflected Luminescence

In mirrored waters, secrets flow,
Reflected whispers, warm and slow.
Through the stillness, light transforms,
Creating patterns in blooming forms.

A dance of colors, vibrant and true,
In every ripple, a world anew.
The moonlight glimmers on gentle streams,
Illuminating the heart of dreams.

From shadows cast, brilliance will rise,
Embracing the night, we analyze.
Each sparkle tells a tale of grace,
In this canvas, we find our place.

As the dawn breaks, reflections fade,
Yet memories linger, never betrayed.
Together we breathe, in this sacred glow,
Reflected luminescence, soft and slow.

With every heartbeat, we create the light,
In shared existence, our spirits ignite.
So we venture, through night and day,
In reflected luminescence, forever stay.

Waves of Togetherness

In the glow of twilight's sigh,
We walk hand in hand, side by side.
Each wave whispers tales from the sky,
In our hearts, love's tide will abide.

The moon paints memories on the sea,
As laughter dances with the foam.
Together we sail, just you and me,
Finding our way, together, home.

With every crash, the ocean sings,
A melody of dreams and trust.
Each ripple carries what love brings,
In the embrace of salt and dust.

The stars bear witness to our heart,
As constellations weave our fate.
In this moment, we are a part,
Of a universe, we resonate.

So let the tides pull us ever near,
In this dance, we lose all fear.
Each wave a promise, crystal clear,
Our love's the ocean, vast and dear.

United by the First Light

When dawn breaks with a gentle kiss,
Awakening dreams in the mist.
Our hearts unite in quiet bliss,
Bound by the sun's golden tryst.

The horizon speaks in hues so bright,
As shadows fade, we come alive.
In morning's glow, we find our light,
Together we flourish, thrive, and strive.

With each soft ray that paints the day,
Hope blossoms in the early morn.
United, we let worries sway,
For in this light, new paths are born.

Hand in hand, we greet the dawn,
With dreams aglow, we will explore.
In the warmth of sunlight's yawn,
We stand as one, forevermore.

Through challenges and joys we share,
Our souls entwined, we'll always fight.
'Til evening comes, and stars declare,
We'll cherish every first light.

Celestial Embrace

Under the stars, our spirits soar,
In velvet skies of midnight's grace.
Each twinkle pulls us to explore,
Caught in this cosmic, warm embrace.

Galaxies swirl in dreams we seek,
As whispers of starlight gently swirl.
With every pulse, our hearts grow weak,
In the vastness, we twirl and unfurl.

The moon watches over with silver beams,
Guiding our steps on this endless night.
In every shadow, we weave our dreams,
Together, we shine, embracing the light.

A dance of planets, a rhythm divine,
We lose ourselves in this stellar spree.
In your arms, I know I'm aligned,
Bound to you, eternally free.

So let the cosmos sing our song,
With voices that echo through the abyss.
In this celestial waltz, we belong,
Finding forever in a moment's kiss.

The Light Gathers

As the sun sinks low, shadows grow,
Yet within us, a bright ember glows.
Together we stand, letting hope flow,
In the gathering light, our love knows.

The horizon blushes in hues of gold,
Painting our path in warmth and grace.
In this embrace, stories unfold,
With every heartbeat, we find our place.

Stars emerge as daylight wanes,
Whispers of dreams wrapped in the night.
In tenderness, love softly reigns,
In the stillness, we hold on tight.

With the dusk, our journey begins,
As the moon unveils its silver glow.
In the quiet, true love never dims,
Together we rise, together we grow.

So as the world fades into the dark,
In the depths, our flame shall stay bright.
With every breath, we leave a mark,
In the gathering light, we ignite.

Song of the Sunlit Sky

In the sky, sunbeams dance,
Whispers of warmth, a golden chance.
Clouds drift softly, dreams take flight,
In the embrace of morning light.

Birdsongs echo, sweet and clear,
Nature's symphony, all we hear.
Colors awaken, bright and bold,
Tales of beauty waiting to unfold.

Mountains stand with grace so grand,
Rivers flow, a gentle hand.
Fields of flowers sway and play,
In the heart of the sunlit day.

Winds carry laughter, joy in the air,
Moments of wonder, free from care.
Leaves rustle softly, secrets shared,
Together in silence, souls laid bare.

As daylight fades, colors ignite,
Sunset whispers, bidding goodnight.
In the twilight's soft embrace,
We find our peace, our sacred place.

Nature's Canvas of Companionship

Beneath the sky, we sit and dream,
Nature paints in vibrant stream.
Each leaf a story, each flower a smile,
Together we wander, mile by mile.

The brook sings softly, a watery tune,
Holding our secrets under the moon.
In the rustling grass, we find our song,
In the arms of nature, we truly belong.

The tall trees whisper, sharing their lore,
With each gentle breeze, they open the door.
Hand in hand, we tread this land,
United in beauty, together we stand.

Mountains tower, steadfast and wise,
Reflecting our hopes in the broadening skies.
As stars emerge, our dreams take flight,
In nature's embrace, all feels right.

With every sunrise, our hearts align,
In nature's canvas, our love will shine.
Through seasons' change, we'll carry on,
In this world of wonder, our spirits drawn.

Painting Our Future in Light

With palettes bright, we seek to create,
Visions of tomorrow, we celebrate.
Brushes in hand, we paint the skies,
A future unfolding, where hope flies.

Colors blend softly, dreams intertwine,
In every stroke, our spirits align.
The canvas whispers, urging us near,
As we craft a world, vibrant and clear.

Each layer tells stories, brave and bold,
Of laughter, of love, and tales retold.
In shades of passion, we find our way,
Building our dreams, day by day.

From twilight's embrace to dawn's first light,
We shape our path with courage and might.
Together we'll rise, side by side,
In this masterpiece, we take pride.

The future awaits, a canvas so wide,
With hearts as our brushes, we won't hide.
In every moment, we'll find our place,
Painting our journey with love and grace.

Together at the Break of Day

At dawn's first light, we share a glance,
The world awakens, a brand new chance.
Together we greet the sun's warm rise,
In the gentle morning, love never lies.

With every step, we embrace the dew,
Paths of possibility, waiting for two.
Whispers of nature, sweet and clear,
In the quiet moments, we draw near.

Colors bloom forth, a vibrant array,
Hand in hand, we seize the day.
The horizon beckons, calling our names,
In this shared journey, nothing remains the same.

As the sun climbs higher, shadows fade,
In each other's presence, we're unafraid.
With hearts as one, we rise and play,
Together we shine at the break of day.

In laughter and joy, our spirits soar,
Facing the world, we ask for more.
Together in dreams, we'll forge a way,
In love's sweet embrace, come what may.

Radiance in Togetherness

In a circle of light, we stand,
Hearts entwined, hand in hand.
Laughter echoes, pure and bright,
Together, we ignite the night.

Moments woven, soft and sweet,
In this bond, we find our beat.
Each story shared, a spark aflame,
In unity, love knows no name.

Through trials faced, we rise above,
In each challenge, we find our love.
Shadows fade with hope's embrace,
In togetherness, we find our place.

Eyes reflecting dreams untold,
In our hearts, a treasure of gold.
With every glance, a promise made,
In this dance, we'll never fade.

As dawn breaks over the horizon,
In our hearts, a joyous risin'.
Radiance shines, ever bright,
Together, we are the light.

Chasing the Daybreak

Waking whispers of the dawn,
In golden rays, our dreams are drawn.
We chase the sun, with open hearts,
Each day begins, a brand new start.

Steps upon the dew-kissed grass,
In every moment, life's truths pass.
With laughter ringing through the air,
We find our way, beyond despair.

Clouds above, a canvas wide,
Brushstrokes of hope, green fields reside.
With every breath, a wish set free,
Chasing daybreak, you and me.

Through valleys deep and mountains high,
Together we'll reach for the sky.
With every dawn, a fresh embrace,
In this journey, we find our place.

As sunlight spills on the waking land,
In our hearts, the warmth we stand.
Chasing daybreak, hand in hand,
Together, a promise so grand.

The Warmth We Share

In the quiet glow of evening,
With whispers soft, our hearts are leaning.
A gentle breeze, the stars align,
In this moment, your hand in mine.

Fireside tales weave through the night,
The warmth we share, a pure delight.
With every word, a bond we build,
In this space, love is fulfilled.

Embers dance, flickering bright,
Casting shadows, a soft light.
With every laugh, with every sigh,
In this warmth, we learn to fly.

Time slows down, the world fades away,
In this embrace, we choose to stay.
No words needed, a silence sweet,
In our hearts, we feel the beat.

As night deepens, stars appear,
In this moment, all is clear.
The warmth we share, a sacred flame,
Together we rise, never the same.

Luminous Threads

Stitched in dreams, a vibrant hue,
Luminous threads weave me and you.
Each moment cherished, gently sewn,
In this tapestry, love has grown.

Colors blend, through joy and pain,
Every strand tells a story's gain.
With hands that weave, our paths entwine,
In every thread, your heart is mine.

Through darkest nights, we shine so bright,
Guided by the stars, our endless light.
With every twist, a new design,
In this creation, our spirits align.

Together we craft, with gentle care,
Luminous threads, beyond compare.
With each embrace, a stronger bond,
In this fabric, we are fond.

As years unfold, our tale unfolds,
In this journey, love ever holds.
With every stitch, we find our way,
Luminous threads, come what may.

Two Souls at Daybreak

In the hush of morning light,
Two souls awaken, hearts in flight.
With whispers soft, they take a chance,
As shadows fade, they start to dance.

The horizon blushes, colors blend,
As dreams of night begin to mend.
Hand in hand, they're not alone,
In the warmth, their love has grown.

Each promise made in silent vow,
Two lives connected, here and now.
With every breath, the world aligns,
In the stillness, love defines.

As nature stirs, so does their fate,
Together strong, they contemplate.
The rise of sun, a brand new start,
Two souls entwined, a work of art.

In daybreak's glow, they find their way,
Navigating through the light of day.
A journey crafted, side by side,
Two souls united, love their guide.

Luminous Threads of Connection

In the weave of morning bliss,
Luminous threads, a gentle kiss.
The fabric of their hearts draws near,
In every glance, love crystal clear.

Sunlight dances through the leaves,
As time unfolds, the heart believes.
With every stitch, a bond they share,
An unseen force that draws them there.

The world awakens, colors bright,
Illuminated by their light.
In laughter's echo, joy takes flight,
Two souls connected, pure delight.

As morning blooms, they breathe as one,
A tapestry beneath the sun.
Each moment stitched, they hold so tight,
In the warmth of love, they find respite.

Together, they blaze a trail so bold,
With threads of silver and strands of gold.
In every heartbeat, they reaffirm,
Two souls in harmony, love will burn.

Synchronized as the Sun Rises

Softly dawn begins to break,
Two hearts in rhythm, dreams awake.
With synchronized steps, they align,
In morning's glow, their love will shine.

At the edge of day, they take a breath,
In the silence, conquering death.
As waves of color sweep the skies,
Their love unfurls, it never dies.

In every heartbeat, they find their song,
Two souls together, where they belong.
With the sun's ascent, they soar above,
In this new light, they find their love.

Through whispers shared and laughter bright,
They embrace the warmth of golden light.
Synchronized as the sun does rise,
Two souls dance in the morning skies.

In the tapestry of day ahead,
They'll weave the dreams that love has fed.
As morning's grace unfolds anew,
Two souls in sync, forever true.

Dawn's Gentle Caress

Dawn whispers softly through the trees,
A tender touch carried on the breeze.
Two souls embraced in morning's glow,
As sunlight spills with a golden flow.

With every ray that meets their skin,
They feel the warmth, the dance begins.
In laughter shared, the world awakes,
A symphony of love that gently breaks.

The sky adorned in hues so bright,
Casts shadows long, in soft twilight.
Together they wander, hand in hand,
In this moment, a promised land.

Each heartbeat echoes nature's song,
In dawn's caress, where they belong.
With eyes entwined, they seek the day,
Two souls united, come what may.

As the sun rises, hopes ignite,
In its gleam, they find pure light.
With love's embrace, they greet the morn,
In dawn's gentle caress, they're reborn.

Unveiling the Horizon

At dawn, whispers creep through the trees,
A soft glow ignites, the world to seize.
Clouds dance lightly, painting the sky,
Each color a promise, as night waves goodbye.

Mountains stand tall, guardians of light,
Echoing tales of dreams taking flight.
The ocean reflects the sun's warm embrace,
A tapestry woven with time and space.

Hearts awaken to nature's sweet song,
Together in rhythm, we all belong.
Pulsing with life, the earth starts to play,
We tread on this canvas, come what may.

Eyes set on futures unfurling wide,
Trusting the path where hopes coincide.
In every shadow, a beacon shines,
Guiding us forth as our fate aligns.

The horizon beckons, a call to arise,
With courage, we chase the infinite skies.
Here we stand, with dreams intertwining,
As one, we embrace the world, redefining.

Harmony of Dawn

The sun breaks softly, a tender embrace,
Awakening whispers across every space.
Birds chirp melodies, sweet and clear,
In every note, a promise draws near.

Flowers unveil their paintbrush delight,
Colors exploding in morning's soft light.
Dewdrops shimmer, like diamonds they gleam,
Reflecting the wonder, igniting a dream.

Breeze carries secrets from far away,
Inviting our souls to dance and to play.
Nature's orchestra, in perfect accord,
Reminds us of beauty, a heavenly cord.

As shadows retreat, the day claims its throne,
Harmony found in the light we've outgrown.
Together, we rise, hand in hand with fate,
In the dawn we unite, celebrating our state.

With each new sunrise, our spirits ignite,
Embracing the dawn, our futures are bright.
In unity's arms, we gather and stand,
The promise of harmony, forever our band.

Interwoven Spirits

In the weave of life, our threads intertwine,
Stories echo softly, a design so divine.
Connected by laughter, sorrow, and grace,
Each spirit a beacon, lending its face.

Through trials and triumphs, we find our way,
Support in the silence, more than words say.
Like rivers that meet, our paths align,
In the heart of our essence, a love so fine.

Hands joined together, we march with pride,
Facing the storm, side by side we bide.
In moments of stillness, we gather our might,
Interwoven as one, we shine ever bright.

Across every distance, our souls will sing,
A melody of unity, love is the spring.
In whispers of twilight, our hopes will soar,
Transcending the night, forever we explore.

With courage and trust, we venture forth wide,
Embracing the journey, hearts open wide.
Through the fabric of time, together we soar,
Interwoven spirits, forevermore.

Rise of the Collective

From the ashes of old, new voices arise,
With the strength of the many, we reach for the skies.
Bound by a purpose, we stand ever tall,
In unity's grasp, we answer the call.

Together we gather, crafting our dreams,
Painting the future in vibrant streams.
Each spark a reminder of power combined,
Awakening visions that once were confined.

In cities and gardens, our hopes intertwine,
Building up bridges, like old bottles of wine.
Our laughter resounding, a symphony loud,
Echoing through, as we gather the crowd.

Through struggles and hardships, our spirits entwined,
Embracing our differences, one of a kind.
Resilient and strong, we rise hand in hand,
The beauty of many, our own promised land.

Transcending division, we see eye to eye,
In the rise of the collective, we reach for the sky.
With hearts that are open, we honor our pact,
In this dance of togetherness, nothing subtracts.